Taylor Margaret

Stay Fit Mom Meal Prep Cookbook

Contents

    1.

    2.

    3.

    4.

    5.

    6.

    7.

    8.

    9.

    10.

1

Chapter 1: Introduction to Healthy Meal Prep

In this inaugural chapter of "Stay Fit Mom Meal Prep Cookbook," we embark on a journey that goes beyond mere culinary prowess. We delve into the profound realm of healthy meal preparation and its transformative impact on your well-being. You'll discover that meal prep is not just a culinary skill; it's a lifestyle choice that can empower you to make healthier eating decisions, save time, and provide a structure that's invaluable for individuals with memory care needs.

The Importance of Meal Prep

To truly appreciate the significance of meal prep, we must first recognize its profound impact on our daily lives. Meal prep is the practice of planning, preparing, and portioning meals ahead of time, often for an entire week. It isn't merely a trendy buzzword; it's a strategy that can revolutionize your relationship with food and nourishment.

Picture this scenario: it's a hectic weekday evening, and you've just arrived home from work, tired and hungry. The prospect of cooking a nutritious meal from scratch feels daunting, and the allure of takeout or processed convenience foods becomes all too tempting. This is where meal prep enters the scene as your culinary savior.

By dedicating a portion of your time each week to meal prep, you gain several noteworthy advantages:

Time Savings: With prepped meals, you can have a wholesome, homemade dinner on the table in mere minutes. No more last-minute grocery store runs or agonizing over what to cook.

Consistent Nutrition: Meal prep allows you to control the ingredients, portion sizes, and nutritional content of your meals, ensuring that you consistently meet your dietary needs.

Budget-Friendly: Eating out or ordering takeout regularly can take a toll on your finances. Meal prep, on the other hand, is budget-friendly, as it often involves buying ingredients in bulk and minimizing food waste.

Health Benefits: With meal prep, you have the power to craft balanced, nutrient-dense meals that support your health goals, whether that's weight loss, muscle gain, or simply maintaining a healthier lifestyle.

Reduced Stress: Knowing that your meals are prepped and ready to go can alleviate the stress and decision fatigue that often accompanies mealtime, which is particularly beneficial for those with memory care needs.

Now, let's emphasize the significance of meal prep for individuals with memory care needs. Dementia, Alzheimer's disease, and other memory-related conditions can introduce unique challenges when it comes to eating and nutrition. Memory care patients may forget to eat, lose interest in food, or face difficulties with mealtime coordination. Meal prep can be a vital tool in addressing these challenges.

Meal Prep for Memory Care Needs

When catering to individuals with memory care needs, certain meal prep strategies can be incredibly helpful:

Routine and Consistency: Establishing a regular mealtime schedule is crucial for individuals with memory care needs. Consistency helps create a sense of familiarity, making it more likely that they will remember to eat.

Finger-Friendly Foods: Some memory care patients may struggle with utensils or have difficulty swallowing. Preparing meals that are easy to eat with fingers or minimal utensil use can be beneficial.

Color and Texture: Incorporating a variety of colors and textures in meals can stimulate appetite and make the dining experience more enjoyable for individuals with memory care needs.

Small, Frequent Meals: Instead of three large meals, consider breaking the day into smaller, more frequent meals and snacks. This approach can help ensure adequate nutrition, especially if appetite is inconsistent.

Labeling and Reminders: Labeling prepped meals with clear, large-font names and reheating instructions can assist memory care patients in independently accessing their meals.

In this chapter, we'll delve deeper into these strategies and provide you with practical tips and recipes tailored to the unique needs of individuals with memory care needs. We believe that meal prep can not only nourish the body but also nurture the soul, and we're excited to guide you on this enriching journey towards healthier, more mindful eating.

2

Chapter 2: Getting Started with Meal Planning

In the second chapter of the "Stay Fit Mom Meal Prep Cookbook," we embark on the essential first steps of your meal prep journey: the art of meal planning. This chapter is a cornerstone, setting the stage for successful meal prep. Whether you're a novice or a seasoned cook, we will guide you through the process of creating a weekly meal plan that is not only delicious and nutritious but also tailored to the unique dietary and memory care needs of your loved ones.

Assessing Your Dietary Needs

Before you dive into meal planning, it's vital to assess your dietary needs and goals. This step is crucial for individuals with memory care needs, as it ensures that each meal provides the necessary nutrients and supports their overall health. Here's a detailed breakdown of how to assess dietary needs:

Consultation with a Healthcare Professional: For individuals with memory care needs, it's advisable to consult with a healthcare professional or a registered dietitian who specializes in memory-related conditions. They can provide valuable insights into specific dietary requirements and restrictions.

Determine Daily Caloric Needs: Calculate the daily caloric needs of the person you're caring for. Factors such as age, gender, activity level, and any underlying medical conditions should be considered. This will serve as a foundation for portion control.

Nutrient Focus: Identify key nutrients that should be prioritized in the diet. These may include Omega-3 fatty acids, antioxidants, and foods rich in vitamins and minerals that support brain health.

Texture and Consistency: If the individual has difficulty swallowing or chewing, discuss texture modifications with the healthcare professional. Soft, pureed, or minced foods may be necessary to ensure safe and comfortable eating.

Allergies and Sensitivities: Take note of any allergies or food sensitivities that the individual may have. Avoiding allergenic ingredients is paramount.

Favorite Foods and Preferences: Inquire about the person's favorite foods and preferences. Tailoring the meal plan to include these items can make mealtimes more enjoyable.

Once you've gathered this information, you'll have a clear understanding of the dietary needs and preferences to consider when planning meals. Remember, every individual is unique, and a personalized approach is key, especially for those with memory care needs.

Creating a Weekly Meal Plan

With dietary needs and preferences in mind, it's time to create a weekly meal plan that strikes a balance between nutrition, variety, and practicality. Here's a step-by-step guide:

Set Clear Goals: Define your meal planning goals. Are you aiming for weight management, improved cognitive function, or simply ensuring regular, nutritious meals? Setting clear objectives will guide your choices.

Start with Staples: Identify staple ingredients that can be used across multiple meals. For example, whole grains like rice, quinoa, and pasta, as well as lean proteins like chicken, tofu, or fish, can form the foundation of your meals.

Build Balanced Meals: Each meal should ideally include a source of lean protein, vegetables, and whole grains. This balanced approach provides a variety of nutrients and flavors. For individuals with memory care needs, this balance can be adjusted as necessary, with a focus on softer textures if needed.

Plan for Snacks: Don't forget about snacks. Nutrient-dense snacks can help maintain energy levels throughout the day. Consider options like yogurt, fruit slices, or smoothies.

Prep Ahead: Identify which components of meals can be prepared in advance. For instance, you can chop vegetables, marinate proteins, or pre-cook grains. This reduces cooking time during the week.

Include Variety: Aim for variety in your meal plan. Incorporate different proteins, vegetables, and grains to prevent monotony and ensure a wide range of nutrients.

Portion Control: Use the calculated daily caloric needs to determine appropriate portion sizes. This is especially crucial for those with memory care needs, as overeating or undereating can have significant implications for health.

Consider Dietary Restrictions: If there are dietary restrictions or allergies, plan meals that adhere to these requirements. There are often creative ways to accommodate specific needs without sacrificing flavor.

Weekly Grocery List: Compile a comprehensive grocery list based on your meal plan. Organize it by sections to make shopping efficient.

Flexibility: Be open to adjustments. Sometimes, preferences change, or there may be unforeseen circumstances. Flexibility ensures that mealtimes remain stress-free.

Incorporating Memory Care Strategies into Meal Planning:

Texture Adaptations: If the individual has difficulty with regular textures, explore soft or pureed versions of their favorite dishes. Soups, stews, and mashed vegetables can be excellent options.

Finger Foods: If fine motor skills are a concern, consider finger foods that are easy to grasp and eat. This can enhance independence during mealtimes.

Color and Presentation: Pay attention to the visual appeal of the meal. Colorful and visually enticing dishes can stimulate appetite and make mealtimes more enjoyable.

Regular Reminders: Establishing a routine for mealtimes can help ensure that the individual with memory care needs remembers to eat. Use alarms or verbal reminders as needed.

In this chapter, we've laid the foundation for successful meal planning that not only meets dietary needs but also considers the unique challenges of individuals with memory care needs. As you progress through this journey, remember that meal planning is not rigid; it's adaptable and should always prioritize the well-being and comfort of those you're caring for.

3

Chapter 3: Essential Kitchen Tools and Ingredients

In this pivotal chapter of the "Stay Fit Mom Meal Prep Cookbook," we explore the indispensable elements of the culinary world: kitchen tools and ingredients. Whether you're an aspiring chef or someone stepping into the kitchen for the first time, having the right tools and ingredients at your disposal is crucial. We'll not only guide you through the essential items but also discuss how to adapt them to the specific needs of individuals with memory care challenges.

Must-Have Kitchen Equipment

Let's begin by diving into the world of kitchen equipment. These tools are the building blocks of your culinary journey, and selecting the right ones can significantly impact the ease and efficiency of your meal prep. For individuals with memory care needs, simplicity and user-friendliness are key considerations. Here's a comprehensive list of must-have kitchen equipment:

Cutting Boards: Opt for large, sturdy cutting boards with non-slip grips. Consider color-coded boards for separating foods and preventing cross-contamination.

Knives: A good set of knives is essential. Look for sharp, comfortable handles and blade covers for safety. For those with limited dexterity, there are adaptive knives designed with larger, ergonomic handles.

Pots and Pans: Invest in a range of pots and pans, including a non-stick skillet, saucepan, and stockpot. Lightweight options with ergonomic handles can ease the cooking process.

Food Processor or Blender: These appliances are incredibly versatile. They can be used to puree foods, create smoothies, and make soft-textured dishes for those with swallowing difficulties.

Slow Cooker: A slow cooker simplifies meal preparation by allowing you to set and forget your dishes. It's excellent for tenderizing proteins and creating soft-textured meals.

Microwave: A microwave oven is indispensable for reheating and quickly preparing simple meals and snacks.

Baking Sheets and Casserole Dishes: These are essential for oven-baked meals and casseroles. Opt for non-stick options for easy cleanup.

Measuring Cups and Spoons: Precision is key in cooking. Ensure you have a set of measuring cups and spoons for accurate portioning.

Mixing Bowls: A variety of mixing bowls in different sizes can accommodate various prep needs.

Can Opener: Look for an easy-to-use can opener, especially if canned goods are a regular part of your meal plan.

Tongs and Spatula: These tools aid in handling and flipping foods. Choose options with comfortable grips.

Digital Thermometer: For food safety and accurate cooking, a digital thermometer is a must-have. It ensures that meats and other proteins reach the desired internal temperature.

Colander: A colander is essential for draining pasta, vegetables, and other foods.

Food Storage Containers: Invest in a variety of containers for storing prepped ingredients and meals. Ensure they are easy to open and close.

Adaptive Utensils: For those with limited dexterity, consider adaptive utensils with larger, easy-to-grip handles.

Labeling Materials: Labeling tools like markers and labels help identify the contents and dates of prepped items, making mealtime organization easier.

Stocking Your Pantry

Now that we've covered essential kitchen equipment, let's delve into stocking your pantry. Having a well-stocked pantry ensures that you're always prepared to create delicious and nutritious meals. Here's a comprehensive list of pantry staples:

Grains and Cereals:

Rice (white, brown, or specialty varieties)
Pasta (regular or gluten-free)
Quinoa
Oats
Whole-grain bread or wraps
Proteins:

Canned tuna or salmon
Canned beans (e.g., black beans, chickpeas)
Peanut or almond butter
Nuts and seeds (e.g., almonds, walnuts, chia seeds)
Eggs
Canned and Jarred Goods:

Canned vegetables (e.g., tomatoes, corn, peas)
Canned fruits (in water or juice)
Broth or stock (vegetable, chicken, or beef)
Tomato sauce or paste
Olive oil
Vinegar (e.g., balsamic, apple cider)
Herbs, Spices, and Flavorings:

Salt and pepper
Garlic powder or minced garlic
Onion powder
Dried herbs (e.g., oregano, basil, thyme)
Spices (e.g., paprika, cumin, cinnamon)
Low-sodium soy sauce or tamari
Dairy and Dairy Alternatives:

Milk or milk alternatives (e.g., almond milk, oat milk)
Cheese (if applicable to dietary needs)
Yogurt or dairy-free yogurt
Sweeteners:

Honey
Maple syrup
Sugar (regular, brown, or alternative sweeteners)
Miscellaneous:

Baking powder and baking soda
Flour (regular or gluten-free)
Cornstarch
Cooking spray
Canned soups (low-sodium options)
Condiments (e.g., ketchup, mustard, mayonnaise)
Adapting the Pantry for Memory Care Needs

For individuals with memory care needs, it's essential to focus on simplicity, nutrition, and ease of use. Here are some additional considerations when stocking the pantry:

Texture-Modified Foods: Ensure that you have pureed or soft-textured alternatives for items like fruits, vegetables, and proteins. These can be used to create meals that are easier to swallow.

Low-Sodium Options: Opt for low-sodium or no-salt-added canned goods and condiments. Excessive sodium can have negative health effects, especially for individuals with certain medical conditions.

Dietary Restrictions: If the individual has dietary restrictions, such as gluten intolerance or lactose intolerance, stock gluten-free flours, pastas, and dairy-free alternatives.

Familiar Favorites: Include the individual's favorite foods and snacks in the pantry. Familiarity can encourage appetite and make mealtimes more enjoyable.

Pre-Portioned Items: Consider pre-portioned snacks and ingredients to simplify meal prep and ensure portion control.

Labeling: Clearly label items in the pantry for easy identification. Use large, legible fonts, and include any special instructions for preparation.

By thoughtfully stocking your kitchen with these essential tools and ingredients, you'll not only streamline your meal prep process but also ensure that you're equipped to create meals that cater to the specific needs of individuals with memory care challenges. Cooking becomes a more accessible and enjoyable experience when you have the right resources at your disposal.

4

Chapter 4: Breakfasts to Jumpstart Your Day

In the fourth chapter of the "Stay Fit Mom Meal Prep Cookbook," we venture into the realm of morning nourishment with a focus on breakfast. As the adage goes, breakfast is the most important meal of the day, and this rings especially true for individuals with memory care needs. In this chapter, we'll explore a spectrum of nutritious and easy-to-prepare breakfast options that cater to varying preferences and dietary requirements while considering the challenges posed by memory care needs.

Human Fuel: The Importance of Breakfast

Before we dive into the culinary delights, let's take a moment to appreciate the significance of breakfast. It serves as the vital fuel that kickstarts your day, replenishing energy stores, and awakening cognitive functions. This is particularly crucial for individuals with memory care needs, as a nourishing breakfast can enhance mental clarity and mood stability.

Boosting Cognitive Function: Breakfast provides essential nutrients and glucose to the brain, promoting cognitive function. For individuals with memory care challenges, this cognitive boost can be particularly beneficial.

Regulating Blood Sugar: A well-balanced breakfast helps stabilize blood sugar levels, reducing the risk of mood swings and irritability, which can be exacerbated by memory-related conditions.

Encouraging Hydration: Breakfast can be an opportunity to hydrate the body with fluids like water, herbal teas, or juice, which can help with overall well-being.

Promoting Nutritional Intake: Breakfast allows for the intake of important nutrients, such as vitamins, minerals, and fiber, which are essential for overall health and well-being.

Setting a Routine: Establishing a morning mealtime routine can provide structure and predictability, which is comforting for individuals with memory care needs.

Now that we've highlighted the importance of breakfast, let's delve into a variety of breakfast options that are not only nutritious but also adaptable to the specific needs of those with memory care challenges.

Quick and Nutrient-Packed Breakfast Recipes

Oatmeal with Nut Butter and Berries:

Ingredients:
   Rolled oats
   Nut butter (peanut, almond, or sunflower seed)
   Fresh or frozen berries
   Honey or maple syrup for sweetness (optional)
   Technique: Cook oats with water or milk, stir in nut butter for added creaminess and protein, and top with berries. The soft texture is suitable for individuals with swallowing difficulties.
   Greek Yogurt Parfait:

Ingredients:
   Greek yogurt or dairy-free yogurt
   Granola (look for low-sugar options)
   Sliced bananas or berries
   Honey or agave syrup for sweetness (optional)
   Technique: Layer yogurt, granola, and fruit in a glass or bowl. This visually appealing and easily customizable option caters to various dietary needs.

Scrambled Eggs with Spinach and Cheese:

Ingredients:

Eggs

Chopped spinach (fresh or frozen)

Shredded cheese (e.g., cheddar or feta)

Technique: Cook scrambled eggs with chopped spinach and top with cheese. Soft scrambled eggs are ideal for those with chewing or swallowing difficulties.

Smoothie Bowl:

Ingredients:

Frozen fruit (e.g., berries, banana)

Greek yogurt or dairy-free yogurt

Nut butter or avocado for creaminess

Toppings (e.g., granola, nuts, seeds)

Technique: Blend frozen fruit, yogurt, and a creamy element (nut butter or avocado) until smooth. Pour into a bowl and top with your choice of toppings. Smoothie bowls are visually appealing and customizable.

Peanut Butter and Banana Toast:

Ingredients:

Whole-grain bread or gluten-free bread

Peanut butter or almond butter

Sliced bananas

Technique: Spread nut butter on toast and top with sliced bananas. This is a simple yet satisfying option that caters to various dietary needs.

Adapting Breakfast for Memory Care Needs

When catering breakfast to individuals with memory care needs, consider the following strategies:

Texture Modifications: Ensure that breakfast options are soft-textured and easy to chew and swallow. Pureed fruits or vegetables can be incorporated into smoothies or oatmeal.

Pre-Portioned Servings: Pre-portioned servings can simplify breakfast preparation and ensure portion control.

Familiar Favorites: Incorporate the individual's favorite breakfast items to encourage appetite and enjoyment.

Visual Appeal: Use colorful ingredients and garnishes to make breakfast visually appealing. This can stimulate appetite and create a more enjoyable mealtime experience.

Routine: Establish a consistent breakfast routine to provide structure and predictability, which can be comforting for individuals with memory care challenges.

In this chapter, we've explored a range of breakfast options designed to jumpstart your day with delicious and nutritious choices. These breakfasts not only provide essential nutrients but also consider the unique needs of individuals with memory care challenges, ensuring that their morning meal is both enjoyable and nourishing. Breakfast truly is a powerful way to begin each day with energy and vitality.

5

Chapter 5: Lunches to Power Through Your Day

In the fifth chapter of the "Stay Fit Mom Meal Prep Cookbook," we transition from the morning meal to a midday feast with a focus on lunch. Lunch serves as a critical point in the day when nourishment meets the demands of energy and mental alertness. For individuals with memory care needs, crafting well-balanced and appealing lunches is paramount to maintaining their overall well-being. In this chapter, we'll explore an array of lunch ideas that not only fuel the body but also cater to dietary preferences and memory care challenges.

Healthy Lunch Ideas for Work and Home

Lunch is often considered the meal that bridges the gap between breakfast and dinner, providing sustenance and energy to carry you through the day. When preparing lunches for individuals with memory care needs, it's essential to consider nutritional density, ease of consumption, and flavor appeal. Here are some wholesome lunch options:

Chicken and Vegetable Stir-Fry:

Ingredients:
    Chicken breast or tofu
    Assorted vegetables (e.g., bell peppers, broccoli, carrots)
    Low-sodium soy sauce or teriyaki sauce
    Cooked brown rice or quinoa

Technique: Stir-fry chicken or tofu with vegetables and sauce, serve over cooked grains. This dish can be customized to include soft-cooked vegetables for easier chewing and swallowing.

Turkey and Avocado Wrap:

Ingredients:

Whole-grain tortilla or lettuce leaves (for a low-carb option)

Sliced turkey or a plant-based protein option

Avocado slices

Leafy greens

Hummus or Greek yogurt-based dressing

Technique: Assemble ingredients in a tortilla or lettuce leaves and roll up. This provides a balance of protein, healthy fats, and fiber, suitable for various dietary preferences.

Salmon and Quinoa Salad:

Ingredients:

Baked or grilled salmon (flaked)

Cooked quinoa

Mixed greens or spinach

Cherry tomatoes

Cucumber slices

Lemon vinaigrette dressing

Technique: Combine salmon, quinoa, and vegetables, drizzle with dressing. This salad is rich in Omega-3 fatty acids and can be adapted to include softer textures.

Vegetable Soup:

Ingredients:

Assorted vegetables (e.g., carrots, celery, zucchini)

Low-sodium vegetable or chicken broth

Protein source (e.g., lentils, shredded chicken)

Herbs and spices for flavor

Technique: Simmer vegetables and protein source in broth with herbs and spices until tender. This option is ideal for those with swallowing difficulties, as it can be pureed to a smooth consistency.

Egg Salad Sandwich:

Ingredients:
  Hard-boiled eggs (chopped)
  Greek yogurt or mayonnaise
  Chopped celery
  Dijon mustard
  Whole-grain bread or gluten-free bread
  Technique: Mix chopped eggs with Greek yogurt or mayonnaise, celery, and mustard. Spread on bread for a classic and satisfying sandwich.

Crafting Balanced and Flavorful Salads

Salads are a versatile and nutrient-packed lunch option that can be customized to suit a variety of tastes and dietary needs. When preparing salads for individuals with memory care challenges, consider these tips:

Soft Ingredients: Incorporate soft vegetables like cooked carrots, peas, or avocado for easier chewing and swallowing.

Protein Boost: Add a source of protein such as shredded chicken, canned tuna, or legumes for sustained energy.

Dressing on the Side: Provide dressing on the side to allow for personal preferences and portion control.

Texture Modifications: For those with severe swallowing difficulties, consider pureeing the salad ingredients into a softer texture.

Familiar Flavors: Incorporate ingredients and flavors that the individual enjoys to make the salad more appealing.

Color Variety: Use a variety of colorful ingredients to create an aesthetically pleasing salad, which can stimulate appetite.

Wraps, Sandwiches, and Portable Options

When crafting wraps, sandwiches, or portable lunch options, keep these considerations in mind:

Soft Breads: Opt for softer bread options or wraps that are easier to chew and swallow.

Protein Choices: Include protein sources like lean meats, dairy-free protein alternatives, or hummus for a balanced meal.

Finger Foods: Create wraps or sandwiches that can be easily held and eaten with the hands, promoting independence during mealtimes.

Customizable: Allow for customization by including a variety of fillings and condiments, so individuals can tailor their lunch to their preferences.

In this chapter, we've explored a variety of lunch options that cater to the diverse dietary preferences and memory care needs of individuals. Lunch is not just a midday meal; it's an opportunity to nourish the body and mind, providing sustenance and energy to power through the day. These lunch ideas balance nutrition with taste, ensuring that meals are both delicious and supportive of overall   well-being.

6

Chapter 6: Wholesome Dinners for the Whole Family

As the day winds down and evening approaches, the dinner table becomes the center of family gatherings and communal nourishment. In the sixth chapter of the "Stay Fit Mom Meal Prep Cookbook," we explore the world of dinners, where flavors and nutrition converge to create memorable meals. Dinners hold a special place in the hearts of many, and this chapter is dedicated to crafting wholesome dinners that cater to the diverse tastes, dietary preferences, and memory care needs of individuals.

Family-Friendly Dinner Recipes

Dinner is often seen as the main event of the day, where families gather to share not only food but also stories and laughter. Preparing dinners that are both nutritious and delicious is essential, and this becomes even more critical when catering to individuals with memory care needs. Here are some family-friendly dinner recipes that strike a balance between flavor, nutrition, and ease of consumption:

Herb-Roasted Chicken with Mashed Potatoes and Steamed Vegetables:

Ingredients:
    Whole chicken or chicken pieces
    Potatoes
    Assorted vegetables (e.g., carrots, green beans)
    Fresh herbs (e.g., rosemary, thyme)

Technique: Roast chicken with fresh herbs for flavor, serve with creamy mashed potatoes, and steamed vegetables. This classic meal can be adapted with softer textures for those with swallowing difficulties.

Vegetable and Lentil Soup:

Ingredients:

Mixed vegetables (e.g., onions, carrots, celery)

Red lentils

Low-sodium vegetable broth

Herbs and spices for flavor

Technique: Simmer vegetables, lentils, and broth with herbs and spices until tender. This comforting soup can be pureed for a smoother consistency.

Salmon with Lemon-Dill Sauce and Quinoa:

Ingredients:

Salmon fillets

Cooked quinoa

Lemon-Dill sauce (made with Greek yogurt or dairy-free yogurt)

Steamed asparagus or broccoli

Technique: Grill or bake salmon, serve with quinoa, and drizzle with Lemon-Dill sauce. This meal is rich in Omega-3 fatty acids and can be modified for various dietary preferences.

Pasta Primavera:

Ingredients:

Whole-grain pasta or gluten-free pasta

Assorted vegetables (e.g., bell peppers, cherry tomatoes, zucchini)

Garlic and olive oil for flavor

Technique: Sauté vegetables and garlic in olive oil, toss with cooked pasta. This customizable dish can incorporate soft-cooked vegetables for those with swallowing difficulties.

Stuffed Bell Peppers:

Ingredients:

Bell peppers

Ground turkey or plant-based protein

Quinoa or rice

Tomato sauce

Technique: Hollow out bell peppers, stuff with a mixture of ground turkey, cooked quinoa or rice, and tomato sauce. Bake until peppers are tender. This dish offers a balance of protein and whole grains.

One-Pot Wonders for Easy Cleanup

One-pot meals are a blessing for busy families and caregivers, offering convenience and minimal cleanup. Here are some one-pot dinner ideas that cater to memory care needs:

Chicken and Rice Casserole:

Ingredients:

Chicken thighs or chicken pieces

White or brown rice

Mixed vegetables (e.g., peas, carrots, corn)

Low-sodium chicken broth

Technique: Combine all ingredients in a casserole dish, season, and bake until chicken is cooked and rice is tender. This hearty meal can be adapted with softer textures.

Beef Stew:

Ingredients:

Lean beef stew meat

Potatoes

Carrots

Onion

Low-sodium beef broth

Technique: Brown beef, add vegetables and broth, simmer until meat is tender. This comforting stew can be modified by using tender cuts of beef and softer-cooked vegetables.

Vegetarian Chili:

Ingredients:

Mixed beans (e.g., kidney beans, black beans)

Diced tomatoes

Bell peppers

Chili spices (e.g., cumin, chili powder)

Technique: Combine all ingredients in a pot, simmer until flavors meld. This versatile dish can be pureed for a smoother consistency.

Pulled Pork Sandwiches:

Ingredients:

Pork shoulder or a plant-based protein alternative

BBQ sauce

Whole-grain rolls or gluten-free rolls

Coleslaw (optional)

Technique: Slow-cook pork with BBQ sauce until tender, serve on rolls with coleslaw if desired. This finger-friendly meal is perfect for those who prefer to eat with their hands.

Spaghetti with Meatballs:

Ingredients:

Whole-grain spaghetti or gluten-free spaghetti

Lean ground meat or plant-based meatballs

Tomato sauce

Fresh basil for garnish

Technique: Cook spaghetti, heat meatballs in tomato sauce, and serve. This classic dish can be modified with softer textures if needed.

Vegetarian and Vegan Dinner Options

For those who prefer plant-based or vegan dinners, consider these options:

Lentil and Vegetable Curry:

Ingredients:

Red lentils

Mixed vegetables (e.g., cauliflower, bell peppers)

Coconut milk

Curry spices (e.g., turmeric, cumin)

Technique: Simmer lentils, vegetables, and coconut milk with curry spices. This flavorful curry can be pureed for a smoother texture.

Tofu and Vegetable Stir-Fry:

Ingredients:

Extra-firm tofu

Assorted vegetables (e.g., broccoli, snap peas)

Stir-fry sauce (look for low-sodium options)

Cooked brown rice or quinoa

Technique: Stir-fry tofu and vegetables in sauce, serve over cooked grains. Soft-cooked tofu can be used for those with swallowing difficulties.

Mushroom Risotto:

Ingredients:

Arborio rice

Assorted mushrooms

Vegetable broth

White wine (optional)

Technique: Sauté mushrooms, add rice and broth (and wine if using), simmer until rice is creamy. This comforting dish can be adapted with softer-cooked mushrooms.

Adapting Dinners for Memory Care Needs

When preparing dinners for individuals with memory care needs, the following strategies can be helpful:

Texture Modifications: Ensure that dinner options are soft-textured and easy to chew and swallow. Soft-cooked vegetables and tender cuts of meat can be used.

Familiar Flavors: Incorporate ingredients and flavors that the individual enjoys to make the meal more appealing.

Color Variety: Use a variety of colorful ingredients to create visually appealing dishes, stimulating appetite.

Dining Environment: Create a pleasant dining environment with appropriate lighting and minimal distractions to enhance the dining experience.

Family Involvement: Encourage family members or caregivers to join the meal, providing companionship and support.

In this chapter, we've explored a range of dinner ideas that cater to the diverse tastes and dietary needs of individuals while considering memory care challenges. Dinner is more than just a meal; it's an opportunity for connection and nourishment, and these recipes aim to create memorable moments around the dinner   table.

7

Chapter 7: Satisfying Side Dishes and Accompaniments

In the seventh chapter of the "Stay Fit Mom Meal Prep Cookbook," we turn our attention to the often-overlooked heroes of a meal: side dishes and accompaniments. These culinary companions play a vital role in enhancing the overall dining experience, adding depth, flavor, and nutrition to the main course. For individuals with memory care needs, carefully crafted side dishes can elevate their meals, making them not only delicious but also nutritionally balanced. In this chapter, we explore a diverse array of side dishes and accompaniments that are both appetizing and accommodating to specific dietary preferences and challenges.

Elevating the Dining Experience

Side dishes and accompaniments serve as the supporting cast to the main course, providing variety and balance to the meal. Their role goes beyond mere sustenance; they can transform an ordinary meal into an extraordinary dining experience. Here's why side dishes are crucial:

Flavor Enhancement: Well-prepared side dishes add layers of flavor and texture to the meal, making it more satisfying and enjoyable.

Nutritional Balance: Side dishes provide an opportunity to include a wider range of nutrients, ensuring that meals are well-rounded and healthful.

Visual Appeal: Colorful and visually appealing side dishes can stimulate appetite and create an aesthetically pleasing dining experience.

Cultural Diversity: Side dishes often reflect cultural diversity, allowing individuals to explore different cuisines and flavors.

Textural Contrast: Side dishes can offer a contrast in texture to the main course, providing variety and interest to each bite.

Now, let's dive into a world of delightful side dishes and accompaniments that can complement a wide range of main courses and cater to the specific needs of individuals with memory care challenges.

Versatile Vegetable Sides

Vegetables are a staple in side dishes, offering a plethora of flavors, textures, and preparation methods. Here are some versatile vegetable sides:

Garlic Mashed Potatoes:

Ingredients:
Potatoes
Garlic cloves
Milk or dairy-free milk
Butter or dairy-free butter
Technique: Boil potatoes with garlic until tender, mash with milk and butter. Soft textures can be achieved for those with swallowing difficulties.
Roasted Vegetables:

Ingredients:
Assorted vegetables (e.g., carrots, bell peppers, zucchini)
Olive oil
Herbs and spices for seasoning
Technique: Toss vegetables with olive oil, herbs, and spices, roast until tender. Soft textures can be achieved through roasting.

Sautéed Spinach with Garlic:

Ingredients:
Fresh spinach leaves
Garlic cloves
Olive oil
Technique: Sauté spinach with garlic in olive oil until wilted. Spinach offers a tender texture suitable for various dietary needs.

Cauliflower Mash:

Ingredients:
Cauliflower florets
Milk or dairy-free milk
Butter or dairy-free butter
Technique: Steam or boil cauliflower until soft, mash with milk and butter. This is a lower-carb alternative to mashed potatoes.

Grain-Based Accompaniments

Grains are versatile and can be adapted to various dietary preferences. Here are some grain-based accompaniments:

Herbed Quinoa:

Ingredients:
Quinoa
Fresh herbs (e.g., parsley, basil)
Lemon juice for flavor
Technique: Cook quinoa, toss with fresh herbs and lemon juice. Quinoa provides a soft texture suitable for those with swallowing difficulties.

Brown Rice Pilaf:

Ingredients:
Brown rice
Sautéed onions and garlic
Toasted almonds

Fresh parsley

Technique: Cook brown rice, stir in sautéed onions, garlic, almonds, and parsley. This pilaf offers a combination of textures and flavors.

Couscous Salad:

Ingredients:

Whole-wheat couscous

Chopped vegetables (e.g., cucumbers, cherry tomatoes)

Fresh herbs (e.g., mint, cilantro)

Lemon vinaigrette dressing

Technique: Cook couscous, toss with vegetables, herbs, and dressing. Couscous has a soft texture that is easy to modify.

Protein-Rich Sides and Legumes

Side dishes can also be a source of protein and legumes. Here are some options:

Hummus and Veggie Platter:

Ingredients:

Hummus

Sliced bell peppers, cucumbers, and cherry tomatoes

Technique: Serve hummus with a colorful array of sliced vegetables. This is a finger-friendly option that provides protein and nutrients.

Black Bean Salad:

Ingredients:

Black beans

Corn

Chopped bell peppers

Red onion

Lime-cilantro dressing

Technique: Combine black beans, corn, peppers, and red onion, toss with lime-cilantro dressing. This salad offers a satisfying protein and fiber-rich option.

Dips, Sauces, and Condiments

Dips, sauces, and condiments can elevate the dining experience. Here are some flavorful options:

Tzatziki Sauce:

Ingredients:
Greek yogurt or dairy-free yogurt
Cucumber, grated and drained
Garlic
Fresh dill
Technique: Mix yogurt, cucumber, garlic, and dill for a refreshing sauce. Tzatziki can be used as a dip or a topping for various dishes.

Mango Salsa:

Ingredients:
Fresh mango, diced
Red onion
Jalapeño
Lime juice
Technique: Combine diced mango, red onion, jalapeño, and lime juice for a sweet and spicy salsa. This can be served as a condiment or dip.

Adapting Side Dishes for Memory Care Needs

When preparing side dishes for individuals with memory care needs, consider the following strategies:

Texture Modifications: Ensure that side dishes are soft-textured and easy to chew and swallow. Steam or roast vegetables until tender, and use soft-cooked grains.

Familiar Flavors: Incorporate ingredients and flavors that the individual enjoys to make the side dishes more appealing.

Color Variety: Use a variety of colorful ingredients to create visually appealing side dishes, stimulating appetite.

Temperature: Serve side dishes at an appropriate temperature to enhance both safety and enjoyment.

Small Servings: Offer smaller portions of side dishes to prevent overwhelming the individual and promote comfortable eating.

In this chapter, we've explored a wide array of side dishes and accompaniments that can elevate any meal, catering to various dietary preferences and memory care challenges. Side dishes aren't just add-ons; they are integral to creating a complete and satisfying dining experience. These versatile recipes offer opportunities for nutrition, flavor, and personalization, ensuring that every bite is a delight.

8

Chapter 8: Desserts to Satisfy the Sweet Tooth

In the eighth chapter of the "Stay Fit Mom Meal Prep Cookbook," we delve into the realm of desserts. Desserts are the sweet ending to a meal, a treat that brings joy and satisfaction to the palate. For individuals with memory care needs, dessert can be a source of comfort and pleasure. In this chapter, we explore a delightful assortment of dessert options that not only indulge the sweet tooth but also consider dietary restrictions and the unique challenges faced by individuals with memory care needs.

The Role of Desserts in Meal Planning

Desserts are more than just a delicious indulgence; they hold a special place in our dining experiences. Here's why desserts are important:

Sensory Pleasure: Desserts appeal to our senses, providing a delightful contrast to savory flavors and textures.

Emotional Comfort: Desserts often evoke feelings of comfort and nostalgia, making them a source of emotional well-being.

Social Connection: Sharing dessert with loved ones fosters social connections and enhances the overall dining experience.

Nutritional Balance: Desserts can be a source of essential nutrients when prepared with healthful ingredients.

Stress Relief: Enjoying a sweet treat can reduce stress and promote relaxation.

Now, let's explore a variety of dessert options that cater to different tastes and dietary requirements, ensuring that individuals with memory care needs can savor the sweetness of life.

Simple and Satisfying Dessert Ideas

Desserts don't have to be elaborate to be enjoyable. Here are some simple yet satisfying dessert ideas:

Fruit Salad with Honey and Mint:

Ingredients:
  Fresh fruits (e.g., berries, melon, kiwi)
  Honey
  Fresh mint leaves
  Technique: Toss fresh fruits with a drizzle of honey and garnish with mint leaves. This refreshing dessert is rich in vitamins and antioxidants.
  Greek Yogurt Parfait:

Ingredients:
  Greek yogurt or dairy-free yogurt
  Fresh berries
  Granola (look for low-sugar options)
  Technique: Layer yogurt, berries, and granola in a glass. This parfait offers a balance of protein, fiber, and natural sweetness.
  Banana Ice Cream:

Ingredients:
  Ripe bananas
  Vanilla extract (optional)
  Technique: Freeze sliced ripe bananas, then blend until creamy. Add a touch of vanilla for flavor. This dairy-free "ice cream" is a healthier alternative.
  Baked Apples with Cinnamon:

Ingredients:

Apples

Cinnamon

A drizzle of honey (optional)

Technique: Core apples, sprinkle with cinnamon, and bake until tender. Drizzle with honey for extra sweetness. Baked apples are soft and comforting.

Healthier Dessert Options

For those looking for healthier dessert choices, consider these options:

Chia Seed Pudding:

Ingredients:

Chia seeds

Almond milk or dairy-free milk

Fresh fruit (e.g., berries, sliced banana)

Technique: Mix chia seeds with almond milk, refrigerate until it thickens. Top with fresh fruit. This pudding is rich in fiber and Omega-3 fatty acids.

Dark Chocolate-Covered Strawberries:

Ingredients:

Dark chocolate (70% cocoa or higher)

Fresh strawberries

Technique: Melt dark chocolate, dip strawberries, and let them cool. Dark chocolate offers antioxidants, and strawberries add natural sweetness.

Yogurt and Berry Parfait:

Ingredients:

Greek yogurt or dairy-free yogurt

Mixed berries

Crushed nuts (e.g., almonds, walnuts)

Technique: Layer yogurt, berries, and crushed nuts. This parfait balances protein, antioxidants, and healthy fats.

Oatmeal Cookies with Raisins:

Ingredients:

Rolled oats

Raisins

Cinnamon

Technique: Mix rolled oats, raisins, and a pinch of cinnamon, then bake into cookies. These cookies are a source of fiber and natural sweetness.

Adapting Desserts for Memory Care Needs

When preparing desserts for individuals with memory care needs, consider the following strategies:

Texture Modifications: Ensure that desserts have a soft texture that is easy to chew and swallow. Puree or finely chop fruits if needed.

Mini Servings: Serve desserts in smaller portions to prevent overwhelming individuals and promote comfortable eating.

Familiar Flavors: Incorporate flavors and ingredients that the individual enjoys and finds comforting.

Finger Foods: Choose desserts that can be easily eaten by hand, allowing for independence during mealtime.

Visual Appeal: Use colorful fruits and garnishes to create visually appealing desserts that stimulate appetite.

Serving Assistance: Offer assistance with serving and eating desserts as needed, providing support and ensuring safety.

In this chapter, we've explored a range of dessert ideas that cater to different tastes and dietary preferences while considering the unique needs of individuals with memory care challenges. Desserts are a source of joy and comfort, and these recipes aim to provide a sweet ending to every meal, promoting both physical and emotional   well-being.

9

Chapter 9: Snacking Smart for Sustained Energy

In the ninth chapter of the "Stay Fit Mom Meal Prep Cookbook," we shift our focus to the often underestimated but essential aspect of eating: snacks. Snacking can be a valuable part of a well-rounded meal plan, providing sustained energy, curbing hunger between meals, and offering a delightful break in the day. For individuals with memory care needs, selecting and preparing snacks thoughtfully is especially important to ensure their nutritional needs are met. In this chapter, we delve into the world of smart snacking, exploring a variety of options that are not only tasty but also tailored to specific dietary preferences and the challenges faced by individuals with memory care needs.

The Role of Snacks in Meal Planning

Snacking is more than just a between-meal indulgence; it serves several important functions in a meal plan:

Energy Boost: Snacks provide an energy boost, combating fatigue and promoting alertness.

Hunger Control: Smart snacking can help control hunger between meals, preventing overeating during main mealtimes.

Nutrient Intake: Well-chosen snacks can contribute to meeting daily nutritional requirements.

Hydration: Snacks can also serve as an opportunity to increase fluid intake, especially when incorporating hydrating options.

Mood Enhancement: Enjoying a satisfying snack can enhance mood and provide a sense of comfort and pleasure.

Now, let's explore a range of snack options that cater to diverse tastes and dietary requirements, ensuring that individuals with memory care needs can snack smart and enjoy the benefits of well-planned snacks.

Nutrient-Dense Snacks

Nutrient-dense snacks provide essential vitamins, minerals, and energy to fuel the body and mind. Here are some wholesome options:

Greek Yogurt with Berries:

Ingredients:
  Greek yogurt or dairy-free yogurt
  Fresh berries (e.g., blueberries, strawberries)
  Drizzle of honey (optional)
  Technique: Spoon Greek yogurt into a bowl, top with fresh berries, and drizzle with honey if desired. This snack offers protein, probiotics, and antioxidants.
  Trail Mix:

Ingredients:
  Mixed nuts (e.g., almonds, walnuts)
  Dried fruit (e.g., raisins, apricots)
  Dark chocolate chips
  Technique: Mix nuts, dried fruit, and dark chocolate chips for a balanced blend of healthy fats, fiber, and a touch of sweetness.
  Hummus with Baby Carrots:

Ingredients:

Hummus

Baby carrots

Technique: Dip baby carrots in hummus for a satisfying combination of fiber, protein, and vitamins. This snack is also finger-friendly.

Smoothie with Spinach:

Ingredients:

Spinach leaves

Banana

Greek yogurt or dairy-free yogurt

Almond milk or dairy-free milk

Technique: Blend spinach, banana, yogurt, and milk for a nutrient-packed smoothie. Spinach can be pureed for a smoother texture.

Hydrating Snack Options

Staying hydrated is crucial for overall well-being. Hydrating snacks offer a dual benefit of quenching thirst and providing nutrients. Here are some options:

Watermelon Cubes:

Ingredients:

Fresh watermelon

Technique: Cut watermelon into bite-sized cubes for a hydrating and refreshing snack. Watermelon is rich in hydration and vitamins.

Cucumber Slices with Hummus:

Ingredients:

Cucumber slices

Hummus

Technique: Dip cucumber slices in hummus for a hydrating and satisfying snack. This combination provides hydration and fiber.

Coconut Water with Pineapple:

Ingredients:

Coconut water

Fresh pineapple chunks

Technique: Combine coconut water and fresh pineapple for a tropical and hydrating treat. Pineapple can be finely chopped for ease of consumption.

Protein-Packed Snacks

Protein-packed snacks are ideal for sustained energy and muscle support. Here are some options:

Hard-Boiled Eggs:

Ingredients:

Hard-boiled eggs

Technique: Simply peel and enjoy hard-boiled eggs as a portable source of protein and essential nutrients.

Cottage Cheese with Peaches:

Ingredients:

Low-fat cottage cheese or dairy-free cottage cheese

Sliced peaches (fresh or canned in juice)

Technique: Top cottage cheese with sliced peaches for a protein-rich and satisfying snack. Canned peaches can be a convenient option.

Peanut Butter on Whole-Grain Crackers:

Ingredients:

Whole-grain crackers

Peanut butter or almond butter

Technique: Spread peanut butter on whole-grain crackers for a combination of protein and whole grains. This snack can be customized with softer crackers if needed.

Adapting Snacks for Memory Care Needs

When preparing snacks for individuals with memory care needs, consider the following strategies:

Texture Modifications: Ensure that snacks have a soft texture that is easy to chew and swallow. Puree fruits if needed, and choose soft nuts and seeds.

Mini Portions: Serve snacks in smaller portions to prevent overconsumption and promote comfortable eating.

Visual Appeal: Use colorful ingredients and visually appealing presentation to stimulate appetite.

Familiar Flavors: Incorporate familiar flavors and ingredients that the individual enjoys for added comfort.

Hydration Reminder: Encourage fluid intake by offering hydrating snacks like fruits with high water content.

Scheduled Snack Times: Establish regular snack times to provide structure and routine in the daily meal plan.

In this chapter, we've explored a range of snack options that cater to different tastes and dietary preferences, while also considering the specific needs of individuals with memory care challenges. Smart snacking offers a multitude of benefits, from sustaining energy to enhancing mood, and these recipes aim to make snacking a pleasurable and nutritious experience.

10

Chapter 10: Navigating Special Dietary Needs

In the tenth and final chapter of the "Stay Fit Mom Meal Prep Cookbook," we tackle a crucial aspect of meal planning and preparation—meeting the unique dietary needs of individuals with various health conditions and dietary restrictions. It's essential to recognize that not everyone follows a standard diet, and catering to special dietary needs is both a compassionate and necessary endeavor. In this chapter, we will explore different dietary requirements, including diabetes, heart health, gluten-free, and vegetarian diets, while also considering the challenges posed by memory care needs. We'll provide insights, recipes, and strategies to help individuals and caregivers navigate these dietary paths with confidence and culinary creativity.

Understanding Special Dietary Needs

Before delving into specific diets, it's important to understand the significance of catering to special dietary needs. Individuals with various health conditions or dietary restrictions require specific nutrient profiles to maintain health and well-being. Addressing these dietary needs not only ensures better physical health but also enhances quality of life and promotes a sense of normalcy and inclusion.

1. Diabetes-Friendly Eating

The Challenge: Managing blood sugar levels is paramount for individuals with diabetes. A diabetes-friendly diet aims to regulate blood sugar while providing balanced nutrition.

Strategies:

Carbohydrate Awareness: Monitoring carbohydrate intake is key. Focus on complex carbs like whole grains, vegetables, and legumes.

Balanced Meals: Include lean protein, healthy fats, and fiber-rich foods in every meal.

Portion Control: Be mindful of portion sizes to prevent blood sugar spikes.

Recipes:

Grilled Salmon with Quinoa and Roasted Vegetables: This balanced meal provides protein, healthy fats, and complex carbs.

Chickpea and Spinach Curry: Fiber-rich chickpeas and vegetables help stabilize blood sugar.

2. Heart-Healthy Eating

The Challenge: Promoting cardiovascular health involves reducing saturated fats, cholesterol, and sodium while increasing heart-healthy nutrients like fiber and Omega-3 fatty acids.

Strategies:

Choose Lean Proteins: Opt for lean cuts of meat, poultry, or plant-based proteins.

Healthy Fats: Incorporate sources of healthy fats like avocados, nuts, and olive oil.

Salt Reduction: Reduce salt intake by using herbs and spices for flavor.

Recipes:

Mediterranean Quinoa Salad: Loaded with vegetables, olives, and olive oil, this salad promotes heart health.

Baked Chicken Breast with Herbed Couscous: A lean protein paired with whole grains and herbs.

3. Gluten-Free Eating

The Challenge: Those with celiac disease or gluten sensitivity must avoid gluten, a protein found in wheat, barley, and rye, while still maintaining balanced nutrition.

Strategies:

Gluten-Free Grains: Opt for gluten-free grains like rice, quinoa, and corn.

Read Labels: Carefully read food labels to identify hidden sources of gluten.

Vegetables and Fruits: Emphasize naturally gluten-free produce for added nutrients.

Recipes:

Quinoa and Black Bean Stuffed Bell Peppers: A gluten-free twist on a classic dish.

Gluten-Free Banana Bread: A satisfying dessert without gluten-containing flours.

4. Vegetarian Eating

The Challenge: Vegetarians avoid meat and sometimes other animal products, making it essential to find alternative sources of protein and essential nutrients.

Strategies:

Protein Variety: Include a variety of plant-based proteins like tofu, beans, and lentils.

B12 Supplement: Consider a B12 supplement, as it is primarily found in animal products.

Iron and Calcium: Pay attention to iron and calcium intake through fortified foods or supplements.

Recipes:

Chickpea and Vegetable Stir-Fry: A protein-packed, plant-based stir-fry.

Tofu Scramble with Spinach: A protein-rich breakfast option.

5. Memory Care and Special Diets

The Challenge: Individuals with memory care needs may have difficulties with mealtime, requiring adaptations to ensure proper nutrition.

Strategies:

Texture Modifications: Prepare soft-textured foods that are easy to chew and swallow.

Familiar Flavors: Incorporate familiar flavors to enhance mealtime appeal.

Regular Schedule: Establish a consistent mealtime routine for comfort and predictability.

Recipes:

Creamy Butternut Squash Soup: A smooth, easy-to-eat soup rich in vitamins.

Mashed Sweet Potatoes: Soft and flavorful, a source of beta-carotene.

Creating Inclusive Meals

Incorporating special dietary needs into meal planning doesn't mean sacrificing flavor or variety. Instead, it invites creativity and a broader culinary horizon. To create inclusive meals, consider these approaches:

Flexibility: Be open to trying new ingredients and recipes to accommodate different dietary needs.

Variety: Explore a diverse range of foods to ensure that meals remain interesting and satisfying.

Consultation: Seek guidance from healthcare professionals or registered dietitians to tailor meal plans to specific health conditions.

Family Involvement: Encourage family members and caregivers to participate in meal planning, making it a collaborative effort.

Education: Invest time in learning about the specific dietary needs and preferences of individuals to provide personalized and compassionate care.

In this final chapter, we've delved into the realm of special dietary needs, offering strategies, recipes, and insights to navigate the diverse dietary paths of diabetes management, heart health promotion, gluten-free eating, vegetarianism, and memory care considerations. By embracing these dietary journeys with empathy and culinary creativity, we can create meals that promote health, well-being, and inclusivity for all.

11

Conclusion

As we reach the end of the "Stay Fit Mom Meal Prep Cookbook," we hope this culinary journey has been as rewarding for you as it has been for us. Throughout these ten chapters, we've explored the art and science of meal preparation, considering not only the nourishment of the body but also the joy it brings to our lives. Mealtime is more than sustenance; it's an opportunity for connection, pleasure, and self-care.

We've covered a wide spectrum of topics, from mastering the basics of meal prep to creating delicious and nutritious breakfasts, lunches, dinners, snacks, and desserts. We've ventured into the world of specialized diets, catering to the unique dietary needs of individuals with conditions like diabetes, heart health concerns, gluten sensitivity, vegetarian preferences, and the challenges of memory care.

Our aim has always been to empower you with knowledge and inspire you with creativity. We believe that preparing meals is an act of love, whether you're cooking for yourself, your family, or individuals with special dietary requirements. It's an expression of care, an investment in well-being, and a way to create lasting memories around the table.

We want to extend our heartfelt gratitude to you, our readers. Your dedication to the art of meal prep and your commitment to providing nourishing, delicious, and thoughtful meals to your loved ones is truly commendable. We hope that the recipes, techniques, and strategies shared in this cookbook have enriched your culinary repertoire and made meal prep a more enjoyable and manageable part of your life.

Remember that meal prep is a journey, and like any journey, it's not about reaching a final destination but about savoring each step along the way. Embrace the creativity, relish the flavors, and cherish the moments you create around the table. Your commitment to nourishing both body and soul through the magic of cooking is a gift to be celebrated.

As we close this cookbook, we wish you countless culinary adventures, endless moments of joy, and a deep sense of fulfillment as you continue to stay fit and healthy, one meal at a time.

With heartfelt gratitude and warmest wishes,

Taylor Margaret.

Made in the USA
Las Vegas, NV
20 September 2023

77858685R00031